EXPLORERS WANTED!
On Safari
Simon Chapman

EXPLORERS WANTED!

books by Simon Chapman:

In the Jungle

Under the Sea

On Safari

In the Wilderness

On the South Sea Islands

In the Himalayas

In the Desert

At the North Pole

Simon Chapman
EXPLORERS
WANTED!

On Safari

LITTLE, BROWN AND COMPANY

New York ❧ Boston

Little, Brown and Company

Time Warner Book Group
1271 Avenue of the Americas, New York, NY 10020
Visit our Web site at www.lb-kids.com

First U.S. Edition: September 2005

ISBN 0-316-15541-1

First published in Great Britain by Egmont Books Limited in 2003
10 9 8 7 6 5 4 3 2 1
COM-MO
Printed in the United States of America

CONTENTS

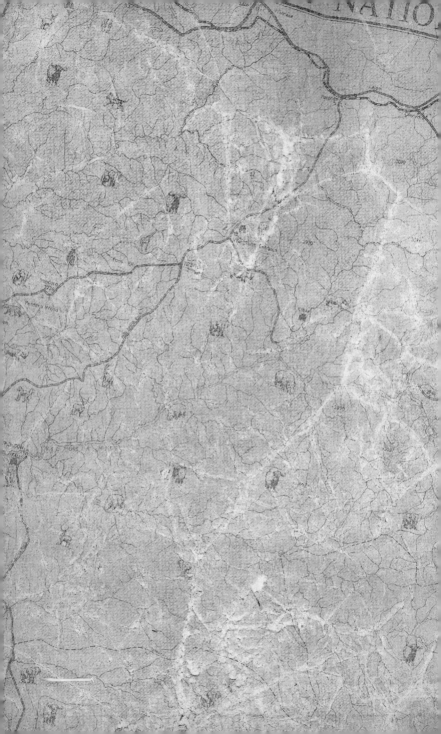

SO ... YOU WANT TO BE A SAFARI EXPLORER?

Want to go to the African savannah where wild beasts roam ...?

Do you want to meet ... **distant** tribes ...?

Find **ferocious** animals ...?

Discover **wonders** of the **natural** world?
If the answer to any of these questions is **YES**,
then this is the book for you. Read on ...

THIS BOOK WILL give you the essential tips on how to travel through the African savannah, such as what to take and what you might find in the bush. There are also some pretty scary true-life stories of some of the people who have tried to explore it before...so read on!

YOUR MISSION...

should you choose to accept it, is to mount an expedition through the African bush to find what the tribes of the interior know as the "Mosai-aa-Tunya" — whatever that is!

The name translated roughly means "The Smoke That Thunders." It is said to be a magical place where the spirits live. No one has travelled there before, though some of the nomadic Mkosi people, who herd cattle in the thorn-scrub beyond the great lake, say that on still days they can hear a deep rumbling sound and that clouds form over the northern hills.

WHAT IS MOSAI-AA-TUNYA?

IS IT THE HOME OF SUPERNATURAL SPIRITS OR SOME FANTASTIC GEOLOGICAL PHENOMENON?

This map sketch might help you —
but only to a point. Once you have
crossed the grasslands to the lake,
you'll be travelling into the unknown.

You'll need to know how to survive
the dangers you meet and how to make
contact with the Mkosi, the only people
who might be able to help you find

"THE SMOKE THAT THUNDERS."

"The Smoke
That Thunders"

Thorn-
bush
country

Swamps

Plains

N
W ✦ E
S

Time to set the scene ...

Let's find out some vital facts about the savannah environment before the mission gets under way.

Well ... It's a pretty big area. Most of Africa, in fact; stretching from Senegal in the west to Kenya in the east and down to South Africa. This is "bush country." You could drive for weeks on end and never get through it and just see grass and trees and rocky outcrops. It's a wilderness and you're going to explore it! But before you set

AFRICA FROM SPACE

off, you'll need some extra information and you'll need to know what to take. There are savannah grasslands in other parts of the world too. They have the same sort of climate and plants, but the animals are very different.

SOUTH AMERICA

AFRICA

AUSTRALIA

SAVANNAH GRASSLANDS

SOUTH AMERICA
Giant anteater
White-tailed deer
Rhea

AFRICA
Aardvark
Kob antelope
Ostrich

AUSTRALIA
Echidna (spiny anteater)
Grey kangaroo
Emu

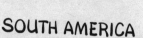

But what's it like in bush country?

The first thing to understand about the savannah is that this is a place with a split personality.

Firstly, there's a DRY season. In fact, most of the year it's dry! Day by day, it gets hotter and hotter. The clouds disappear. The waterholes and the rivers dry up. The ground becomes cracked and the air is full of dust. Animals cluster anywhere there's still a drop of water.

5

Fires start easily and can quickly ravage the grassland. But the roots survive and the grass will soon grow back once the rains come. All the life on the savannah — animals, plants, and people — are waiting for the clouds to return.

Then there's the RAINS — the other half of the split personality. The parched riverbeds are washed through with instant flash floods. Any low-lying land becomes soggy and swampy. The dead-looking grass suddenly bursts into life — and grows and grows.

This is the time of abundance, when the animals give birth to their young. There's more than enough fresh grass and leaves to go around for the plant eaters, and there's more than enough plant eaters to go around for the meat eaters; the lions, hyenas, and hunting dogs. That means there's an awful lot of scraps and dead meat for the scavengers, and one heck of a lot of dung that needs clearing away! What happens to it?

What will you be traveling through?

It's easier to get lost than you might imagine. Maybe not on the really open grassland, but in the bush — the scrub savannah — when you look around you will find that every direction looks the same!

VIEW FORWARD

VIEW BACKWARD

Just bushes ... scraggy-looking trees ... spiky mounds of mud.

The mud piles are termite mounds. They're concrete-hard, made from a mixture of chewed-up soil and termite spit . . . a lot of termite spit. Termites are tiny insects that live in huge colonies rather like ants. There'll be tens of thousands of them scuttling about inside in deep tunnels and chambers, walled in against predators and the hot sun, which would soon dry out their soft, white bodies. There'll be blind, eyeless workers, soldiers to protect them, a few male kings, and one queen, the size of your little finger. She's unable to move; a pudgy, bloated, egg-laying machine. And their food? Dead wood, leaves, and grass; and to make that go that little bit further, a special fungus that lives only on termite poop! As you can imagine, with that mixture, it could get pretty smelly in there so termite towers have hollow tubes going up inside the outer layers that allow air to circulate. These shafts can go several meters under the ground and help to provide a controlled climate for the termites — a sort of insect air-conditioning. There are a lot of these mounds around in the savannah; that means a stupendous number of termites and, in turn, a lot of plants to keep them going.

TERMITE MOUND

As you travel through the bush on your journey, it's worth remembering that it's the termites (and the ants too), not the antelopes, elephants, and zebras, that really shift the plant matter around here.

OK, it's fine admiring the insect architecture, but that's not going to get you through this scrub. You need a route you can walk along. How about a game trail? This is a path where large animals have bashed (and munched) their way through. There are tracks of antelope, and patches where the grass has been worn away by their hooves. There's a fair bit of dung too. And some of it's rolling!

ANTELOPE TRACK

DID YOU KNOW?

Dung beetles stand on their front feet and roll dung with their back legs. They hide it, eat some of it, and lay their eggs in the rest. That's where their grubs grow up.

(How would you like to be raised in a ball of dung?)

You carry on following the game trail. There's something rustling behind the bushes ahead of you. It could be antelopes — or it could be the predators that eat them! (Remember, they also know that animals pass by here regularly.) You creep up, making sure to stay downwind so whatever is there doesn't smell you.

You are downwind of the antelope but upwind of the buffalo. Bad move!

What could be there?

An impala...?

A giraffe...?

A lion...?

It's a flock of goats and a small boy herding them.

Yes, people live here too!

Here's a savannah story about how to travel in style.

Bebe Bwana — "lady boss" — set out on safari from Mombasa to Mount Kilimanjaro in East Africa in 1891. She hired lots of porters to carry all her stuff. This vital equipment included a long blond wig and a silk ballgown, which she wore to impress the chiefs whose lands she was passing through. Forever keeping up appearances, May French Sheldon (which was her real name) did not walk cross-country on her expedition. She rode in a Palanquin (like a sedan chair or wheel-less carriage), which was carried by some of her porters. Sometimes, she slept in it. One night, she woke up to find something catching a ride on top of it — a five-meter long python!

Chapter 1

GETTING READY

NOW TO EQUIP your expedition.... You'll need to think carefully about the stuff you need for yourself and for the vehicle you will be driving.

Basic Bush Equipment

In the past, some people have dressed up in very impractical outfits.

Take the Landers brothers who explored in West Africa in the 1830s. They wore red hunting coats, baggy Turkish pants (for ventilation) and hats as wide as umbrellas. The locals found it hilarious. People would come from miles around just to stare at these two weird foreign guys.

Another explorer, Mary Kingston, a very prim Victorian lady, always wore a full crinoline dress and carried an umbrella. Surprisingly, this rather uncomfortable and impractical get-up probably saved her life when she fell into a spiked pit trap intended for hunting animals.

But what will you need to take?

CAMERA

COMPASS

SUN HAT

PENKNIFE

MEDICAL KIT

LIGHTER

SHIRT

VEST WITH LOTS OF POCKETS

MAPS

BINOCULARS

SHORTS

SLEEPING BAG

WALKING BOOTS

RIFLE

ROLL MAT

TENT

WATER BOTTLE

If you're walking through country where you are likely to encounter large, dangerous animals, someone in your group should carry a gun.

13

Transportation and Porters

If all that equipment seems like rather a lot to take, it's far less than what was taken by your average Victorian explorer. They brought along tables, chairs, rolls of cloth, wire, and beads to trade with the locals, as well as all sorts of other impractical stuff. But they did have one great advantage — they hired hundreds of porters, or *Wangwana*, as they were called, to carry it all.

Motor vehicles hadn't been invented and pack animals, like horses and mules, were out of the question. The dreaded tsetse fly made this impossible as its bite causes sleeping sickness. Horses, mules, and donkeys are particularly badly affected. Some explorers in southern Africa tried using oxen to haul heavy cartloads of provisions, although even these beasts didn't last for very long before they became sick too. A few took camels. Some even tried Indian elephants, but they had trouble finding the right food for these elephants who were used to living in lush Asian jungles rather than parched African grassland. So, most explorers ended up hiring human porters. A typical expedition "caravan" would contain men from several different tribes. Certain tribes had particular types of baggage that they preferred to carry.

The *Wakamba* carried trade goods; wire, beads, and cloth, the *Swahili* carried personal equipment; tents, blankets, and the *Nyamwezi* took food and ammunition.

There could be hundreds of porters on an expedition. On top of the equipment and trade goods they had to carry, the porters also had to lug along all their own food and personal effects. All of this on hazardous trips that could last months or years. Because of this, the porters eventually got organized into a sort of trade union and set limits on the amount of useless stuff that they were prepared to carry.

The Slave Trade

These tribes of porters didn't just set themselves up for the benefit of a few European explorers who passed their way. There was a lot of trade going on in Africa between the coasts and the interior. Cloth, glass beads, and guns were traded for ivory ... and for slaves.

During the 17th and 18th centuries, in West Africa, thousands of people were kidnapped to work the plantations across the Atlantic Ocean in the West Indies and in Brazil. Settlements were raided and burned, villagers captured or killed. Conditions were appalling for the prisoners. They were chained together and forcibly marched to the coast. They spent months on end crammed in the holds of ships and fed little. Not surprisingly, many died.

In East Africa, even while the West African slave trade was being stamped out, Arab traders and some gun traders, took yet more people captive. By the time European "explorers" arrived in the mid-nineteenth century, they often found the locals distrustful or even downright hostile to strangers. The likes of Mary Kingston and the Landers brothers were often exploring places the slavers had already ransacked.

What about your transportation?

To begin with, at least, you won't be needing porters on this trip. You have a vehicle, a battered old four-wheel-drive nicknamed Bessie (seven previous careful owners). Bessie will be great for eating up the great distances across the open grassland and into the thicker thorn-bush, provided you can find some tracks. Sooner or later, though, you may have to leave her and go out and find yourself some local people to help you get to "The Smoke That Thunders."

Gear Up Bessie

Here is what's available at the "Safariquip" expedition outfitters. But you can't take it all. You'd run out of money and, besides, all that weight would have Bessie sinking in the first bit of mud you come across.

CAMOUFLAGE
NETTING

A ROOFTOP TENT

SPARE
TIRE

BULL
BARS

SAND-
LADDERS

SPARE
TIRE

A WINCH

ZEBRA STRIPES

A SPADE AND
PICK AXE

SPARES AND
TOOL KIT

A JERRY CAN
CONTAINING WATER

A JERRY CAN
CONTAINING GAS

Look at the list. Most of the things are essential, but which four are luxuries? (Answer is on page 20)

What about food?

While you've got a vehicle, carrying lots of provisions isn't a problem — you can take cans of food, bottles of drink, fruit. When you start walking, you'll have to take food that is light and easy to carry, and that doesn't spoil. So do as the locals do: take some mealies and jerky.

Mealies
This is corn meal, also called Sadza. This is like lumpy corn-flour. You mix it with water and boil it into a heavy porridge.

Jerky
Also known as biltong, jerky is dried meat — as tough as old leather, but you'll get used to it. Here are some of the flavors available:

- Regular (cow) flavor
- Kudu or other antelope (don't buy waterbuck jerky. Waterbuck meat is said to taste like paintbrush cleaner)
- Zebra
- Ostrich

A KUDU

There's no need to worry that these animals are hunted and that you'll be eating the wildlife that you want to see. In southern Africa, there are special "game" farms where animals like zebras and antelope are kept much like cattle or sheep in America.

So, that's food, a vehicle, and your personal gear sorted out. Can you think of anything else you're likely to need? A guide maybe, a supply of clean drinking water? Hopefully, you'll find what you want somewhere out in the plains. You're going to get very lost and thirsty if you don't!

ANSWERS from page 18

All the equipment for Bessie is essential except for:

Zebra stripes — But you have to admit they do make Bessie look the part.

Netting — You're not trying to hide!

Bull bars — For the likelihood of hitting an animal by accident, these are probably not worth the extra weight.

Rooftop tent — Not strictly necessary as you already have a tent.

Other things to consider taking are:

- An extra fuel tank
- A metal plate welded to the bottom of the truck to stop damage from rocks in the road
- A friend with another four-wheel-drive. This is worth seriously considering. You can help each other out of trouble. (Unfortunately this is not an option that is available to you on this trip.)

Chapter 2
SETTING OUT ACROSS THE PLAINS

YOU'RE IN BESSIE, the four-wheel-drive, speeding along a bumpy dirt track, sending clouds of dust billowing out behind you. The road is concrete-hard, baked by the sun.

For the first few hours, there are power lines along the edge of the road and on top of these sit hawks and small eagles that occasionally swoop down to catch mice in the yellow grass. Ahead, the land is pancake-flat and the heat haze makes everything shimmer and look slightly wobbly. Where are all the animals you've heard about — the elephants and rhinos, the warthogs and the zebras? Not here. This is cattle pasture, not that there are many cows around, except for some dots in the distance, clustered in the shade of a flat-topped acacia tree. And ahead, what are those?

ANKOLE CATTLE

HAWK

A flock of ostriches speeds off into the scrub as you drive nearer. They've been feeding on the small melon-like fruit that grow in the channels on either side of the road where the water runs off when it rains.

As your journey continues . . .

you pass by villages of small, round mud huts with conical thatched roofs. As you drive farther into the plains, these settlements become less and less frequent and more and more spaced apart. It's harder to find the road too. Now there are just two lines of bare earth where the tires of trucks have worn the grass away. In places, tracks veer off toward villages that lie beyond the bushes to the left and right.

Occasionally, you pass women carrying plastic or clay jugs on their head. But what are they carrying in them?

WATER!

There's no tap water out here. All drinking water comes from the village well. But there's no electricity to pump it up. That has to be done by hand. If you want to fill up your supplies, you'll have to wait your turn in line. At least you can take your water away in your four-wheel-drive. These women will have to carry it all the way home. For some it might be miles to travel, so they will eagerly accept any offer of a lift!

This is Mary Wagatemba. You've offered her a ride in Bessie. She speaks a little English and explains she is returning to her village by the lake after visiting a friend. The lake is about a three days' drive from here.

"The Smoke That Thunders." Oh yes, she's heard of that. She thinks it's somewhere in the thorn-bush country beyond the lake.

She can take you across the lake in her father's boat if you like. **Hakuna matata!** That's Swahili. It's not her main language, she explains. It's just one that everyone knows a little bit of so that people from the different tribes can communicate.

"Hakuna matata" means "No worries!"

You probably know some more Swahili, but never knew it.

Safari – Journey
Daktari – Doctor
Simba – It's a lion, of course!

Here are a few other words you might need later in your journey …

Jambo – Hello
Asante – Thank you
Ndiyo – Yes
Hapana – No
Kifaru – Rhino
Fisi – Hyena

Tembo – Elephant
Kiboko – Hippo
Twiga – Giraffe
Nyani – Baboon
Chui – Leopard
Mbog – Buffalo

Stesheni ya treni – Train station
Mimi ninatoka … – I come from …
Mimi nataka kununua … – I want to buy …
Mimi nataka kwenda … – I want to go to …

As you drive out of the village, Mary sits up front in the four-wheel-drive, pointing out which are the best tire tracks to take across the grass. Watch out for deep holes, she tells you. There are some real axle-breakers dug by aardvarks looking for ants then hollowed out by warthogs making their homes.

AARDVARK

By late afternoon, you figure you've made another 20 kilometers. It's time to set up camp. You find a nice clear area. It looks like it's been trampled by lots of hoofs. You bash down some of the grass at the edges and set up your tent. The ground is too hard to hammer your tent pegs in without them bending, so you tie your tent's guy ropes to some rocks and a knobbly mound of hard earth.

Night falls quickly this close to the equator. By quarter to seven, it's already dark. You had to put your camp up quickly and you may have made some basic mistakes. This is what your campsite looked like when you turned in for the night.

25

Try to spot what mistakes have been made. Match the labels on the picture on the previous page with the hint and the danger.

	HINT	DANGER
1. Campfire still smoldering	A. Termite mounds	P. Hyena
2. Knobbly rock	B. No stones surrounding it	Q. Might start bush fire
3. Shoes left outside tent	C. Attracts scavengers	R. Termites could eat tent
4. Animal tracks	D. There could be a game trail crossing your camp	S. Watch out for scorpions
5. Food (meat) left out	E. Nice, snug hiding place	T. Puff adder
6. Long grass	F. Good "cover" for snakes	U. You could be trampled by animals passing during the night

(Answers on page 27)

Best-case scenario

You wake up in the morning.
Another fantastic African dawn.
Everything is covered in a layer of dew.
The early morning rays of sunlight are
slanting over the savannah, highlighting the shiny,
turquoise feathers of the glossy starlings that are flying

overhead. There is a flock of guinea
fowl pecking the ground around
your camp. Everything is peaceful.
Everything is calm.

Worst-case scenario

You wake up in the morning. A wind whipped up during the night,
sending up sparks from the embers of your fire that set the bush
ablaze. The antelopes and zebras that use this game trail were
frightened into stampeding over your tent. A hyena, attracted by
the scent of the meat you left out, decided that your arm, which
was sticking out of the termite-nibbled wreckage of your tent,
would make a far better meal.

When you felt it bite and hastily pulled your arm back into cover, you heard a hiss and felt a moist, forked tongue flicker over your face. You are sharing your sleeping bag with a poisonous puff adder. So it's your choice. Stay in the tent with the snake or go out and face the hyena.

You were lucky this time. Your camp is intact. Everything's fine – or is it?
Which hazard was not mentioned in the worst-case scenario?

(Answer on page 30)

Luckily, any snakes that are in the grass are too sluggish and dozy in the cool morning dew to bother striking you. You cook up some breakfast, pack up your tent, and drive off into the savannah once again.

Chapter 3
BLOOD-SUCKERS AND THE GREAT MIGRATION

TWO DAYS LATER.

Midday. It's hot, dry and dusty as usual. You're having a break from the driving, resting in the shade of some Mopane trees — and you get bitten. It's just a fly — a big, black fly, like a horsefly — but it packed a nasty bite, and where it has stung soon begins to swell up raised and red. It's bleeding a little too. Ouch! You are bitten again. Mary is swatting around her face, then she rushes back into the Landrover, slams the door, and hastily starts winding up the windows.

"TSETSE!," she shouts.

The scorpion in your shoe.
You must remember to
shake out any unwelcome
"guests" before you
put them on.

You dive into the car as well and for the next five minutes frantically swat all the flies that have followed you in. Soon, the inside of the windscreen and doors are littered with squashed tsetse flies.

Tsetse flies – the scourge of the African bush

They have special pointed mouth parts for puncturing through thick animal hides. To them, your thin human skin is no problem — you are an easy target. These flies feed on blood, but their bites can carry sleeping sickness germs. Sleeping sickness mainly affects cattle, but it can affect people too. However, most of the wildlife in the savannah is immune to the disease.

A TSETSE FLY

The tsetse fly is one reason why there is still wildlife, like elephants and antelope, wandering over large areas of Africa, and not people with farm animals.

Tsetse flies are attracted to large, dark areas — like the hides of cows and buffaloes. In some places, black and blue screens, laced with insecticide, are put up to attract tsetse flies and kill them. Incidentally, some scientists have put forward the idea that zebras have stripes, not to camouflage themselves in long grass, but because the black and white bands confuse tsetse flies and prevent attack.

CLOSE UP

31

ANOTHER NASTY BLOOD-SUCKER...
The Tick — An Aggravating Arachnid

Try walking through the grasslands and you might "pick" these up. Sometime later, you'll feel itching or notice what looks like tiny dark grapes stuck to your legs. They are ticks — small creatures related to spiders — that bury their spiked mouths into you and suck your blood. The danger to you — the bites itch and can get infected. They can cause diseases like "tick typhus."

A TICK

To remove a tick, pull it straight out. It's best to pluck it out using tweezers and not to twist it, as the tick may leave its mouth parts behind, which can cause the area to get infected. Yuck! Some people put a blob of Vaseline on ticks that are stuck in firmly. This makes them back out of the skin, so they can breathe and makes them much easier to extract.

Oxpeckers

Oxpeckers provide a de-ticking service for animals like giraffe and buffalo, which let them peck at all sorts of places to get the ticks out – in the ear, up the nostrils, under the tail! Ow!

Little do the poor beasts know, the oxpeckers are taking advantage of the situation! Sometimes,

they just peck through the animals' skin or open up wounds just to get a good slurp of blood for themselves.

Setting off again ...
sore with Tsetse fly bites ...

Now you're getting farther into the plains, you're starting to see lots of zebras and gazelles. Occasionally, you spot the predators that hunt them, the cheetahs, lions, and hunting dogs.

You don't see nearly as many predators as prey. Here's why.

1. The predators are likely to remain hidden, skulking out of the way. They don't want their prey seeing them and being scared off.

2. To feed each cheetah or hunting dog, there has to be around ten to twenty gazelles. Think about it. If there was just one gazelle for one cheetah, then pretty much all the gazelles would be eaten straight away. If there were just two and one were killed, then how would it breed? Add a couple more gazelles to make up for the fact that disease might get some and several more for luck; the numbers of gazelles start adding up.

This is called a
food pyramid

Ten kilograms of cheetah, fed by 100 kilograms of gazelle, fed by 1000 kilograms of grass. That makes cheetahs the top of this food chain

Grass → Gazelle → Cheetah

However, there is one herbivore (plant eater) that hasn't been mentioned yet. These really are the lawnmowers of the savannah. Along with the zebras, they migrate in their millions to where the grass is greener. After they've been by, the head-high grass is mown flat.

They are ... **the wildebeest!**

BUILD A WILDEBEEST...

Take the front end of an ox ... and the back end of an antelope ... with the mane of a lion ... and the beard of a goat. Add a horse's tail ... and some attitude ... then you have ... a super herbivore.

OX

ANTELOPE

WILDEBEEST

HORSE

LION

GOAT

"We eat far more grass, but nobody notices us."

The Great Wildebeest Migration

Wildebeest move to where the grass grows best. In East Africa, from July to October, up to two million wildebeest (as well as zebras and gazelles), trek thousands of miles from the Serengeti plains in Tanzania north eastward to the Masai Mara in Kenya. They follow the rainfalls, mowing down the lush green grass that springs up immediately after the downpours before moving on again. By January and February, the wildebeest are back in the southern Serengeti giving birth to their young (a bumper time for predators). Then they're off again and the whole cycle continues.

Other grazing animals make similar migrations. In the Sudan, the white-eared kob antelope "follow" the freshest grass, much like the wildebeest. Until recently in southern Africa there was a mass migration of springbok gazelle. Alas — not anymore. Fences put up to prevent buffalo passing on diseases to farmers' cattle blocked their route and so much meat on the hoof was too good an opportunity for hunters to miss. The springbok were wiped out, so only a fraction of their former number remained.

Chapter 4
MUD

IT'S CLOUDY, GRAY and overcast.
There's a definite nip in the air and a stiff
breeze is rippling through the grass.
The swallows that normally catch flies high
in the sky are flitting about just above ground
level. Even the plants seem to know there's a storm coming;
there's a leafy, cut-grass smell in the air. You drive on through
the morning, spotting herds of gazelle and zebras as you
venture further away from "civilization."

By mid-afternoon, the first drops of rain are falling, spattering
the dust on the road. Then, without any warning, it starts
to pour down. The sky blackens. Forks of lightning strike
the ground some way ahead of you. Your windscreen wipers
are going full speed, but can't clear water away fast enough.
You drop the four-wheel-drive into a lower gear.

The wheels are sliding. The dust on top of the road has become like an oily mud-slick. Underneath, the surface is still rock hard, and you slip right across the road more than once as you swerve to avoid rocks. At one lower area where the road dips down, you lock your brakes and skid. The truck hits soft mud and stops dead. The wheels are spinning, but all they are doing is digging you in deeper. You are up to your axles and water is trickling past as the dip becomes a stream. What's more, as the water rushes past Bessie's wheels, it's scooping away the mud on the downstream side and your vehicle is starting to tip over alarmingly!

Get Your Truck Out of the Mud!

1. Look at the gear you equipped your four-wheel-drive with (page 18). Think of the three items you could most do with now?

2. What is your most immediate danger?

A. A lightning strike
B. A flash flood
C. An animal attack

3. You need to free your truck quickly. Match the letters with the numbers below.

A. Find a fixing point for the winch.	1. The flood waters could get worse.
B. You have to work quickly.	2. Use the tree.
C. Use your sand-ladders.	3. Slide these under the wheels if you can.
D. Get the wheels to grip over a larger area.	4. Be careful near to the trees.
E. Watch out for lightning.	5. Let the tires down.

(Answers on page 42)

By the time you've got Bessie out, you're soaked to the skin, covered in mud and thoroughly worn out. It's too wet and too close to nightfall to continue today.

You can't light a fire, as everything is soaked. You spend a miserably damp night curled up on the front seat with just a few soggy biscuits to eat. But lucky you got the vehicle out. The stream is more like a raging river now!

You wake up to the *brip-bripping* sound of frogs. The puddle nearby is full of fish. Storks and cranes have flown in to feast on the food bonanza. Yesterday, this was dried-up savannah. So where have the fish come from?

STORKS

CROWNED CRANE

A. Were they hibernating?

B. Have they wriggled their way over from the stream?

C. Have they flown there?

D. Were their eggs in the ground ready to hatch as soon as it rained?

E. Did the fish have lungs to breathe out of water?

(Answers are on page 44)

ANSWERS from page 40

Give yourself one point for each correct answer.

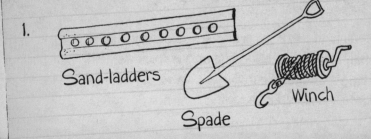

1.

Sand-ladders

Spade

Winch

2. B.

Right now, a flash flood poses an immediate danger as it could wash away your vehicle or could knock tree trunks and branches into it and cause considerable damage. A lightning strike to your vehicle will not harm you (even with you inside) and an animal attack is unlikely.

3. A. 2   B. 1   C. 3   D. 5   E. 4

YOUR SCORE

1 – 4 Useless. If a flash flood didn't wreck or wash away your car, head for home right now. You're obviously not cut out for this type of expedition.

5 – 6 Not too bad. It's all very well acting quickly, but you have to think too!

7 – 9 Well done. We'll make an explorer of you yet! Winch and push Bessie out of the mud.

Actually both A and E are correct.

These fish are called "lung fish." When the pool dried out, they hibernated in the mud at the bottom. They made a hole and covered the inside in a layer of spit that set hard. So did the mud. The lung fish breathed through a small hole at the top, using their lungs. When it rained months later, they wriggled free and started breathing underwater through their gills again.

Driving on in the four-wheel-drive is hard going now. The road is just a mass of soggy mud and if you counted up all the time you spent freeing it from getting stuck, you work out you could have walked quicker. Mary says her village is near. You can leave Bessie there. The four-wheel-drive will be safe. Mary can row you across the lake and into the swamps on the other side in her father's canoe and from there you'll be able to carry on on foot to "The Smoke That Thunders."

Chapter 5
INTO THE SWAMP

MARY WABATENGA'S VILLAGE is by the side
of a long lake that stretches into the distance on either side.
Looking at your map, you can see that going around it would
take ages and would probably be very difficult in Bessie with the
ground so soft after the rains. Your best option is to go across
the lake and then continue on foot.

Mary's village is just a small collection of round
huts with grass thatched roofs. There are
some fields of millet — a grain a bit like corn —
behind the houses, but mostly the people here
look to the lake for their food.

MILLET

Several canoes made from dug-out tree trunks are lined up on the water's edge and alongside, drying out in the sun, are some large fishing nets.

The fish the local people catch belong to a group called "cichlids." Nearly all the fish that live in the lake evolved from one cichlid ancestor that somehow arrived when the lake first formed several million years ago. Since then different types of cichlid have developed to fill all the different fishy lifestyles you can get. These are some of the various types. . . .

SNAIL NIBBLER —
plucks snails off water weeds

ALGAE SUCKER —
down-turned rasping mouth

BIG MOUTH CARNIVORE —
predator

MALAWI EYE BITER —
you can guess what
its favorite
food is!

This is how the situation has been for millions of years. Until recently. Someone decided that boring, little cichlids didn't provide enough nourishment, so they introduced the Nile Perch, which doesn't actually come from the River Nile, nor is it a Perch! These can grow up to one meter long and have an appetite to match. For cichlids! In the great lakes of central Africa, many types are now dying out as the Nile Perch are eating them.

NILE PERCH

Paddling across the lake ...

It's cool out on the water, though the paddling is hard going as the breeze is against you. You watch fish eagles swooping down for fish and, in the distance, you see squat, dark heads of hippos bathing. Once in a while, one opens its mouth in a huge yawn (or maybe to show he's the meanest hippo boss).

You decide it's best to steer the canoe out of their way. Hippos are well known for attacking boats that come too close. That's one close encounter you could do without!

Some way down the shore where you came from, you can see masses of pink flamingos. These don't live here, Mary tells you. They're from another lake nearby and come here once a day to drink. The other lake is a "soda" lake. It's filled with natural alkali chemicals that would burn your hand if you were to dip it in. The flamingos feed off algae scum that grows in the caustic water there. Their tough legs don't get burned, but they can't drink the "soda" water, and it forms a crust on their feathers, which they have to wash off before it sets hard like rock and stops them from flying.

Paddling on further...

When the wind drops, you decide crossing
the lake and watching the lake life go by
is rather pleasant. Correction... would
be, if it wasn't for the clouds of tiny
mayflies. It's not that these tiny insects
bite, it's just that now and then, you get
engulfed in a cloud of them and they
get everywhere – like in your mouth
as soon as you open it to speak.

PAPYRUS
GRASS

The other side of the lake is a swampy
mass of reeds and papyrus grass. There's
still quite a way to go until you reach dry land,
Mary says. You'll have to find the channels that
wind their way through to the land, and you'll
have to keep a keen eye out for dangers like...

A NILE CROCODILE –
five meters long

TINY WATER SNAILS –
the dreaded Bilharzia

A HIPPO

Actually, it is not the bilharzia snails themselves that are the danger, but the even tinier worms that they carry and then discharge into the water around them. Swimming in this water is unsafe, as the worms can burrow through your skin. First, you get an itchy rash. Later when the worms lay their eggs, you might get a fever or stomach pains. You might have blood in your pee. Sometimes though, you feel absolutely nothing. You'll be feeling as right as rain then *pfzzz* — you've done irreparable damage to your internal organs. You get ill and you die. That's why at Mary's village, no one swims in the lake.

Mary finds a channel quite quickly. It's about four meters wide with high papyrus growing up on either side and floating water weed that limits the space that you can paddle in still further. You feel walled in. Every now and then, Mary taps the side of the mokoro (canoe) with her paddle just so that if there is a hippo nearby it won't be surprised and suddenly rear up underneath the boat. There have been lots of cases of boats being tipped over by angry hippos — and of crocodiles eating the survivors as they tried to swim to the shore.

Paddling through the Papyrus
Test your knowledge on the life of the swamps

1. The sitatunga, an antelope that lives in the swamps, has hooves that are wide and spread apart.

But why are they like this?

A. To spread out the sitatunga's weight over a larger area so it can walk on the mats of floating vegetation.

B. A deadly two-pronged weapon.

C. To click together and attract members of the opposite sex.

2. **Which of these is false?**
   Hippos spent all day in the water . . .

A. To avoid sunburn.

B. To prop up their enormous weight.

C. Because they feed on water weed.

3. **True or False?** Hippos whisk their tails around while they are pooping.

4. **True or False?** Hippos have been known to bite people in half.

5. **Can you identify these birds?**

1.   2.   3.   4.

A. Hammerhead   B. Shoebill

C. Saddle-billed stork   D. Secretary bird

(Answers are on page 53)

Paddling on ... and on

Sometimes you go up channels that end as blocked dead-ends. Occasionally, Mary looks worried. Weeds have grown over some of the channels she remembers going along when she was last here. Eventually, you reach some dry land. Hopefully it's the shore, not just an island. Mary says she isn't sure, but she really must go now if she is to get back through the swamps and across the lake to her village by nightfall.

"For Mosai-aa-Tunya, you must head north to where you see cloud in the distance," she says. "If you can get high enough to see a view, you will always see clouds there." Then, once you have unloaded your backpack and gear, Mary paddles back along the channel. She's nearly out of sight when she remembers one last thing.

"Try to find the **Mkosi** people," she shouts. "I'm sure they'll be able to help."

Her canoe slips out of sight and you are alone. Listening to the squawks and the rustling in the reeds, you hope it's a sitatunga there, not a crocodile, as you decide what to do next.

ANSWERS from page 50-51

1. B.

2. C is false. Hippos come out of the water at night to feed on grass on the shore.

3. True. One good reason never to stand behind one!

4. True. The English explorer Samuel Baker told the story of a Dinka chief who had been bitten in half during an unprovoked attack on his canoe.

5. 1. Saddle-billed stork   2. Hammerhead
   3. Shoebill   4. Secretary bird

Chapter 6
ALONE IN THE THORN-SCRUB

IT'S NEXT MORNING and you slept badly in that soggy, mosquito-ridden swamp and as soon as it was light enough, you made your way to firmer ground. You are stranded in the African bush and you are on your own. You face . . .

Rough terrain . . .
intense heat . . .
lack of water . . .

poisonous snakes . . .
stinging scorpions . . .

hungry lions . . .
bad-tempered buffalo . . .

You've got all these and more stacked against you, if you are going to go forward and get to "The Smoke That Thunders."

Those vultures circling high overhead . . . are they waiting for you to drop? They've obviously already picked clean that antelope skeleton by your feet. Will you be next? Those remains might only be two or three days old, but where's all the rest gone?

Waste recycling — savannah style

Here are some of the disposal squad members. Match each animal with the job description on the next page.

1. White-backed vulture

2. Black-backed jackal

3. Carrion beetle and flesh flies

4. Spotted hyena

A. Picks clean anything left

B. Nibbles and picks off any tasty treats

C. Has bone-crushing jaws so it can eat nearly any part of the carcass

D. The "eye in the sky." Their super-sensitive sight lets them spot any animal that goes down for miles around

(Answers are on page 61)

Pecked at by vultures, nipped by jackals, or scrunched by hyenas? Do you want this to happen to you? Time to think! Just what are your options?

You'll need to carry water and food. You'll need help. You decide to take Mary's advice and head north and find the Mkosi people, but you've somehow lost your compass. How do you find which way is North? Use the sun and your wrist watch.

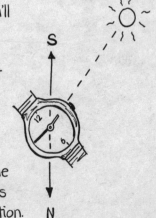

Point the hour hand toward the sun. The line between it and twelve o'clock faces south, so north is in the opposite direction.

If you are in the southern hemisphere, you point the twelve o'clock toward the sun. The line between that and the hour hand points north.

Rather than leaving your lakeside camp with its water supply and setting off now with all your gear, it would be better just to make a short scouting trip, check out the way ahead, see if you can find some Mkosi.

Decide on five pieces of gear that you will need for three or four hours checking the terrain.

WATER
BOTTLE

MACHETE

SOME FOOD

SMALL
MEDICAL KIT

BINOCULARS

CAMERA

COMPASS

SUN HAT

GUN AND AMMUNITION

TENT

Item	Points
Water bottle	**40** Essential
Sun hat	**30** Essential not to get sunstroke
Gun and ammunition	**30** To ward off lions, etc.
Compass	**20** You could use your watch and the sun
Food	**15** No need to take more than just lunch
Machete	**10** You can probably walk around the worst thickets
Small medical kit	**10** A few wound dressings in your pocket should suffice
Binoculars	**5** Not strictly necessary, but could be useful
Camera	**0** Not needed
Tent	**0** This is not a camping trip, just a morning stroll

Your Score

0 — 69   **Hopeless.** Make a signal fire and pray that Mary comes back to rescue you.

70 — 109   **Adequate.** But get your priorities right. This is just a morning's scouting trip into the bush, not a major expedition.

110 — 160   **Excellent.** You're a real explorer in the making. Make sure you practice your Swahili just in case you meet anyone.

Setting off again...

This bush trekking is harder than it looks. The vegetation is out to get you! In particular, the Acacia wait-a-minute bush, which hooks on to your clothes.

Some animals eat this stuff. Giraffes have long, flexible lips and tongues that twist past the thorns to nip off the leaves. Elephants just go for everything — bark, branches, leaves, thorns. The acacia trees take advantage of this. Their seeds are designed to pass all the way through an elephant's gut unharmed.

They plop out at the other end wrapped up in their own ball of fertilizer.

Even the seeds of some of the plants here are vicious. Some have spikes or hooks to catch on to animals as they brush past so they can spread far and wide. The grapple seed of South Africa has gone to extremes!

Some people say that to get through this thorn-scrub, you have to think like a rhino. Get a thick skin. Such a person was the German explorer Karl Mauch who "discovered" (of course, the local Matabele people knew it was there all along!) the lost city of Great Zimbabwe in 1871. He wore a thick suit of ox hide. No thorns could get through, but it must have weighed him down a lot, and boy, how he must have sweated!

BEFORE

AFTER

Peculiar Plants

These are some of the other strange plants you might come across in the thorn-bush...

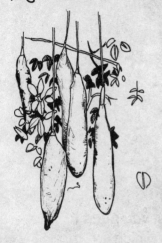

THE SAUSAGE TREE
Those are actually seed pods and, no, you can't eat them.

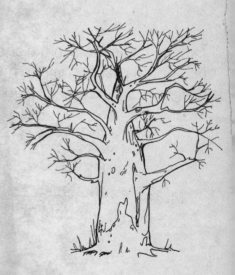

THE BAOBAB TREE
Looks like an upside down tree. Because these are so big and so distinctive-looking, they are good to use as landmarks to make sure you don't get lost.

ANSWERS from pages 55-56

1. D   2. B
3. A   4. C

THE ALOE
One type, the Aloe
Vera, is used in
cosmetic skin products.

But it's the animals in the bush that you need to be worrying about. Time to find out which are the dangerous ones and what you should do if you meet one?

Agitated Animals

Match each animal with what you should do if you encounter it in an ugly mood.

1. Buffalo charging — head down, going for you at full speed.

2. Elephant — ears flapping, head up, trumpeting.

3. Lion — slowly advancing, ears held back.

4. Cobra — rearing up, "hood" of skin on neck open.

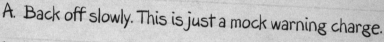

A. Back off slowly. This is just a mock warning charge.

B. Back off slowly, showing as little terror as possible. If it follows, shout at it, or fire a warning shot into the air.

C. Stay perfectly still. Try and shield your eyes, then back off.

D. Climb the nearest tree, or stay still, then side-step at the last moment — it may miss you anyway.

(Answers are on page 64)

ANSWERS from page 63

1. D   You have to bank on the fact that a charging buffalo can't turn all that quickly. Dodging at the last moment is also said to work if a rhino charges at you.

2. A   If the elephant is charging with its head down and ears back, it's time to be really worried, and time to run — like heck!

FULL CHARGE →

3. B   Hope the lion has recently eaten and is not too hungry!

4. C   Some African cobras spit venom at the eyes of animals threatening them. This would be seriously unpleasant and immobilize you if the snake then wanted to give you a (potentially fatal) bite.

Sunset and you're back where you started. Your scouting trip has revealed nothing. You feel as if you're walled in by thorn-bushes. There was a maze of game trails, but you couldn't find one that led away to the North.

You haven't been able to find a place with a view to see if there really are clouds above "The Smoke That Thunders" like Mary said. For that matter, you've still no idea what "The Smoke That Thunders" really is.

Dispirited, you bed down for the night, leaving your fire going to ward off marauding jackals and hyenas.

Chapter 7
MEETING THE MKOSI

WHEN YOU WAKE up, two fearsome-looking men with spears in their hands are standing right above you. But how do you react? Do you shout at them to go away? Run off? Hide under the blankets? Smile your biggest smile and say Hello? Ask for permission to cross their land?

No Reaction

Maybe they don't understand you. You could try some of the Swahili you learned from Mary Wabatenga. For starters, you say Hello — *Jambo*.

Whatever you said, it worked! The faces of the two young men crack into broad smiles. They look at each other and talk quickly. You distinctly hear the words "lost tourist."
"You speak English?" you say.

"Of course," replies one of the Mkosi. **"I'm at college in the capital city. And no, I don't wear my tribal clothes there."** He can see you're staring at his red cloak and beads, and at his friend's long braided hair, which looks to be covered with bright red mud. His face, body, and arms are also smeared with yellowish mud.

"This is my holiday. I'm Nduki. This is Mfasa, my cousin. He's a *moran*, one of the young warriors of the village. He has to stay away until he's proved himself and can come back and become a 'junior elder.'"

67

NDUKI AND MFASA

Nduki goes on to explain that in earlier years, Mfasa would have had to go out and spear a lion to show his worth. Now, he's out with his cousin to explore and learn about "the bush." On this trip, they're really trying to find out if there's any good grazing land in this area for the village's cattle.

"**Mosai-aa-Tunya.**" Nduki says he knows of it. It's beyond their lands, past some rocky outcrops where lots of leopards live. He's been to those hills once and, one morning, when the air was really still, he thought he could hear a deep rumbling in the distance. Maybe that was "The Smoke That Thunders." Nduki and Mfasa are traveling toward the hills. They'll let you tag along with them.

You pack up your stuff and set off. For them, finding their way through the thorn-bush thickets is easy. You make good headway, but in the hot sun, it's thirsty work. Mfasa gives you a swig from his "bottle" — a hollowed-out vegetable called a gourd. *Mmm* — strange taste — it might not be polite to show you don't like it.

"**It's cow's blood mixed with milk,**" Nduki says.

"But don't worry," he adds, "we didn't have to kill the cow. We just bled a little bit off from the jugular vein in its neck. It takes hardly any time to recuperate."

In return for the drink, you offer them a little of the jerky (dried meat) you packed at the start of the trip. Nduki and Mfasa are pleased to accept it, but surprised when you say it's beef. It's a type of meat they don't eat very often even though the people in their village raise cattle.

"What about burgers? Beef steaks?" you ask.

Nduki looks horrified. "Our cattle aren't for killing," he says. "Cattle are like money. The more you have, the richer you are. For us, killing cows to eat would be like you setting fire to ten-dollar bills!"

Some time later...

Hmmm...? You've come across some yellowy-green footballs made of twigs and shredded bits of bark. But what are they? Elephant poop, says Nduki. He points out several other signs that elephants have been around. Several of the trees around you have had branches ripped off. The grass underfoot is flattened. Elephants have definitely been here recently... and they might still be close. He crouches down to investigate further and picks up one of the poops.

ELEPHANT DUNG

Oh, no! Is he really doing that?

Nduki's got one of the football poops in both hands and he's breaking it open like it was a big bread roll. **"A couple of hours old,"** he tells you. How does he know? It all depends on how dried-up the "spoor" has become.

Dry to the middle. That's an old one. One, maybe two, days.

Wet all the way through...
then you'd better watch out!

SPOOR – that's a tracker's way of saying poop – as well as any tracks and animal signs in general. An experienced tracker can tell all sorts of things from droppings, like which animal made them, what it has eaten, and how long ago it passed by ...

Real trackers look for other signs too. For instance, small antelopes, called dikdiks, mark their territories with scent from a gland under their eyes. And elephants? They rip up trees to eat the bark.

Match the spoor to the animal that made it!

1.

2.

3.

A. Leopard — contains bits of fur and is tapered at one end.

B. Black Rhinoceros — grazes on leaves.

C. Impala — eats grass and some leaves.

AN IMPALA

(Answers are on page 75)

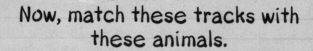

Now, match these tracks with these animals.

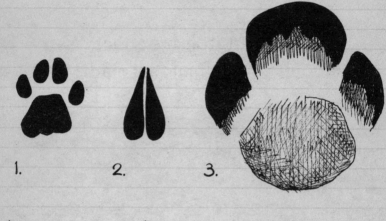

1.

2.

3.

A. Leopard

B. Rhino

C. Impala

(Answers are on page 75)

Yes — Elephants are nearby . . .

In the thorn-bush ahead, you see a trunk wrap around a branch. You hear a tearing and then a scrunching, munching sound — a mother and a calf. It's a bad idea to go this way. Suddenly, behind you a large male stamps out of the bushes. Just look at those tusks! He is huge, and he certainly looks angry. His ears are flapping, and his trunk is raised.

What should you do?

A. Stand still. He won't react if you are not moving.

B. Back off slowly without making a noise.

C. Shout! Clap your hands. Make yourself look as big as possible.

D. Run like mad.

(Answer is on page 75)

These days, seeing a bull elephant with tusks like those is a rare sight. Count yourself lucky. In recent years, thousands of elephants have been poached for their ivory. Gangs of men armed with machine guns go into the bush and shoot up whole herds just to get a few tusks. Rhinos — especially the black variety — have been hunted for their horn to the point where there are only a few hundred left in the whole of Africa. Why? Just because some people think it's lucky to have the handle of their daggers made from rhino horn and other people think that powdered horn will give them a better love life.

73

In some national parks, governments have set up anti-rhino and elephant poaching patrols. Equipped with the latest weapons, jeeps, and spotter-aircraft to stop the poachers, some of these patrols have been very successful — the amount of poaching has been really cut down. But now, there's another problem — too many elephants. Elephants rip up trees. They destroy the thorn-bush savannah, leaving it as open grassland. Then they — and lots of other animals besides — have nowhere to live and feed. It's a real conservation problem. What should be done about it? These are some of the things that are being tried:

- Culling (shooting) elephants, when their numbers outstrip their food supply, and selling the ivory.

- Allowing rich hunters to pay to shoot elephants. The money is then used for nature conservation.

- Tranquillizing a few elephants and taking them by truck to areas where there aren't enough elephants. Unfortunately, this is very expensive and difficult to do. Some say the money would be better spent making the national parks bigger. But then, what happens to the people that already live and farm in these areas? They have a right to the land too!

ANSWER from page 67

A. Correct — You said, "I want to go to Mosai-aa-Tunya," though "Mosai-aa-Tunya" is in a different language. Let's hope they understand.

B. This means, "I want to buy a rhinoceros."

C. This means, "I've come from the train station."

ANSWERS from page 71

1. C   2. B   3. A

ANSWERS from page 72

1. A   2. C   3. B

ANSWER from page 73

B. — Remember, when an elephant starts flapping its ears, it means that it is giving you a warning, trying to scare you off before it really gets annoyed. Any other answer — then it's time to give up this expedition and turn back, that is if you survived the full, head-down charge that would have come next!

The trek continues...

Mfasa and Nduki walk with you for three days, guiding you through the monotonous, brown thorn-scrub as the land slowly rises away from the lake. This is some of the food they find for you along the way....

Termites

Eating insects may take some getting used to, but these ones are very nutritious. Unlike ants, which have to be cooked to destroy their formic acid injected when they bite, termites can be eaten raw. Try hitting the ground around termite mounds with sticks and pouring some water into the holes. The termites think it's raining, then come out. Alternatively, you can put a stick into a hole in a termite mound and pull it out with all the termites that try to bite it.

Roots and tubers

Found by digging around in the soil around certain plants.

A monitor lizard

Pried out of a hole in a tree.

Honey

Your guides collected that by following a small gray bird called a honey guide. It kept calling (a sound somewhat like a box of matches being shaken) and each time you followed it, the crafty bird flew on ... and on ... until finally you reached a bees' nest in the crook of a tree. Nduki and Mfasa made fire and smoked the bees out, and you all feasted on honey while the bird got the wax and the bee grubs that it likes to eat!

NDUKI MAKING FIRE BY HAND-SPINNING A SOFT WOOD STICK IN A NOTCH IN A HARD WOOD BRANCH

Honey guides more often enlist the help of ratels — also known as honey badgers — to help them get into the bees' hives.

Sometime after you've licked the last of the honey from the honeycomb, Nduki says quietly that it's time for him and Mfasa to leave now. The hills are just ahead and, as you haven't found any good pasture for their cattle, they really ought to be heading back toward their village and continuing their search. Before the two Mkosi leave, Nduki points out the way you should go.

Long ago, he tells you, the ancient people of the land, the San bushmen, used to live here. Maybe their rock paintings will show you how to get to "The Smoke That Thunders."

Chapter 8
THE ROCKY KOPPIES

FOUND ALL OVER Africa, lumpy hills of weather-resistant boulders stick up from the plains. Some are rounded, while others have had the outer layers eroded away, leaving mounds of rubble, narrow gullies and caves. The Dutch Afrikaans settlers in southern Africa called these rock formations "koppies."

These are some of the creatures that live amongst the koppies . . .

Ground hornbill
A turkey-sized terror bird.
They mainly hunt lizards and snakes.

Klipspringer
They balance on the tips
of their hooves as they
bound from rock to rock.

Hyrax
Though this animal looks rather like
an oversized hamster, it is in fact
most closely related to the elephant.

Spring hare
A giant type of
kangaroo rat.

Black eagles

These birds ride the up-drafts of hot air, swooping down on hyraxes that aren't keeping a good enough look-out.

The koppies are also home to baboons. You soon learn never to leave your backpack open or have food lying around your camp. Once baboons come to learn that you can provide them with an easy lunch, they will do anything to get hold of your supplies. You should be able to scare them off, but watch those teeth, and look out for the baboon's expression — it might give you a clue as to what it is going to do next.

This baboon's checking you out. Is that explorer as much of a sucker as he looks?

WHITE EYELIDS, BLINKING AT YOU

Slightly annoyed.
A good idea to back off.

HEAD DOWN, FROWNING

Mouth open means "Look at my enormous fangs. I will bite you if you come any closer." He probably won't, but do you want to risk it?

HEAD BOBBING UP AND DOWN

I DIDN'T DO IT. IT WASN'T ME. HONEST.

Cute expression with eyes wide open and eyebrows up. Humans make the same expressions.

An expression you might see on the faces of the young baboons, especially if they are being bullied by the bigger ones.

The reason for these expressions is communication. Baboons live in large groups. They forage around for seeds, leaves, insects, and anything edible they can find (they love trash heaps at the edges of towns). Everyone in the group has to know their place and everyone has to know who's boss.

So why do baboons have bright pink bottoms?

There are two reasons...

1. All baboons have bare patches of skin, tough like the soles of your feet, that they sit on.

2. A bright pink bottom on a female baboon is considered very attractive among the males. No accounting for taste!

Carrying on . . .

The easiest way to walk through the rocks, you soon find, is to follow the course of a dried-up valley that winds between house-sized boulders and overhanging cliff walls. The ground is peppered with the tracks of klipspringers and other small antelopes. Occasionally, you hear the rasping cough of some animal. The cough seems to be keeping up with you . . . following you . . . hunting you? Whatever is making the noise always stays out of sight.

You notice that some of the more sheltered rock overhangs have pictures drawn on them in rust red, black, white, and yellow ochre — natural colors. There are stick men and animals, stripes, and spots. The pictures are thousands of years old. They were drawn by the original inhabitants of Africa, the San (or Bushmen) and show the animals they used to hunt. Over the years, the San were driven out by other tribes who spread through Africa.

Now, only a few remain deep in the Kalahari Desert, where they continue their way of life, hunting animals with spears and arrows, and gathering edible roots to eat.

Eventually, you reach a wide, overhanging rock wall, covered in ancient paintings. At first, it looks like you can go no farther, but looking carefully you can see there are three choices, A, B, or C.

Now you have to decide from the pictures and clues which way leads to Mosai-aa-Tunya.

Think what "The Smoke That Thunders" really is...

· Mary Wagatemba mentioned clouds and rainbows.

· Nduki told you about a deep rumbling sound.

Is Mosai-aa-Tunya . . .

A. An active volcano?

B. A thunderstorm with lightning that starts a bush fire?

C. A huge waterfall where a raging river plunges over the end of a cliff?

Choose a path to take . . . A, B, or C?

Beware! You might find something else – something dangerous if you take the wrong route. Look at the spoor around the entrance to the openings. Use the knowledge you have already gathered to help you with your answer.

(Answers are on page 88)

ANSWERS from page 87

A. Didn't you read the signs! Those were big cat tracks . . . and that was the poop of a carnivore. There is no way through here, nor any sign of the volcano that the picture showed. There is just a cave that is barely large enough for you to stand up in. You hear that cough again, and it's right by your ear. There's no time for your eyes to adjust to the darkness. You're alone with a hungry leopard. I wouldn't like to be in your shoes now!

B. You worm through the gap in the rocks — past a rather agitated porcupine who shoots a couple of quills at you — and you emerge into a valley full of antelope and giraffe. It's a magical place for sure.

There's a deep rumbling sound. Maybe you've found Mosai-aa-Tunya? No, the noise is behind you. The passage has caved in. There's lots of wildlife just as the bushman painting told you, but now you're stuck here. Good luck.

C. You followed the waterfall picture. You worm through the gap upward onto a sunlit plateau. The air rumbles with rolling thunder. A rainbow shimmers in the mist beyond the bushes in front of you. Somehow you know this is it. This is Mosai-aa-Tunya. It's just beyond those bushes in front of you. You rush forward eagerly ... then stop. Oh, no ... Lions! What do you do now?

You are standing right in the middle of a group of three lions. Two of them are lionesses but they aren't any less fierce. They actually do most of the hunting.

You weigh your options.

Chapter 9

"THE SMOKE THAT THUNDERS"

FOR A MOMENT time seems to stand still. Neither of the lions move. One, the male, is apparently asleep. A lioness to your side was feeding off a zebra carcass. Her mouth and chin are stained red with its blood. Now she is motionless, staring at you. Out of the corner of your eye you can see a second lioness. She is making a low purring, growling sound.

Everything depends on what you do now!

Match the option with what you think will probably happen.

A. Shoot at one of the lions.

B. Shoot several shots into the air, shout, and wave your arms around.

C. Try not to look scared and back off quietly.

D. Climb the tree.

E. Run for it!

1. Hopefully this will scare them off.

2. It might work. The lions might not be hungry anyway.

3. Bound to attract their attention even more.

4. Stupid. You might miss or just wound them. A wounded lion is even more dangerous.

5. This is no defense against lions.

(Answers are on page 98)

Whew! Close shave. You back off behind some bushes and make as much ground between you and the lions as possible. The rumbling sound is still there, just as loud and so deep you feel it through your whole body and through the ground, which almost seems to be shaking. The leaves of the bushes ahead ripple, caught by gusts of wind that you can't feel, and the air beyond shimmers as minute droplets of water catch in the sun's rays.

Mosai-aa-Tunya — that must be it!

You push forward through some bushes and hold on! Grip tight before you go right over the edge!

"The Smoke That Thunders."

The name sums it up pretty well. Thousands of tons of water are plunging over the edge of this huge waterfall every second. The roar rumbles around the gorge and echoes around the cliffs. The spray hangs in the air as a fine mist, lighting up as a rainbow where the sunlight hits it.

The real Mosai-aa-Tunya is better known as Victoria Falls, or at least that's what you'll see it called in European and American atlases.

In 1855, the Scottish explorer, David Livingstone, thought it was such a magnificent place that he named it after Queen Victoria, who was the ruler of Great Britain at the time. This is the same Doctor Livingstone as in "Doctor Livingstone, I presume." The explorer Henry Stanley was sent by *The New York Herald* to look for him after he had been "lost" in the African bush for over a year. When Stanley found him at Ujiji in present-day Tanzania, in 1871, those were the famous words he said. At least that's what Stanley wrote in the paper. He probably really said something entirely different.

What a discovery! You got there — against all the odds! The lions, the hippos, tsetse flies, the mud, the heat, and the dust. Will you be like Livingstone and rename the waterfalls and see that name in all the atlases of the world, or will you let them stay as they are — Mosai-aa-Tunya . . .

"The Smoke That Thunders!"

When you get home, will you return to fame and fortune? Maybe your face will be on all the papers and magazines.

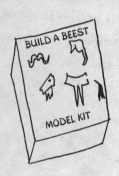

Maybe you'll be given your own TV show to come back and "rediscover" the wonders of the African savannah.

Just one thing though — should you be taking all the credit? After all, you wouldn't have got there without help from Mary Wagatemba and the two Mkosi boys, Nduki and Mfasa.

It's like in the old days of African exploration. Who's ever heard of Sidi Bombay? He managed the caravans of porters and guided the explorers, Livingstone, Speke, and Burton on many expeditions, yet because he never wrote books or gave lectures about his trips, he never became famous. He never got any credit, though he probably "explored" more of Africa than any of them.

Anyway, back to reality. It may have escaped your notice now that you are a great explorer, but do you actually know where you are? You may have driven across the plains, canoed the swamps, been prickled in the thorn-scrub, but do you know how to get back? If you are going to bathe in all that fame and glory, you have to return (alive) to tell the story.

On the following page is a map showing where you've been. Work out which hexagons you will have to go through to retrace your route.

WARNING: You have not visited all of the places on the map.

HINTS: You'll need to re-cross the rocky koppies to the bush country where you met the two Mkosi. Use the baobab tree as a landmark to retrace your route back through the thorn-scrub and across the lake to where Bessie, the four-wheel-drive, is stuck in the mud. The wildebeest are still on their migration, so you'll have to drive past the herds on your way back to the village and the good road at the start.

(Answer is on page 99)

It's time to head home until the next adventure. You've proved you're an expert at exploring the African Bush ON SAFARI, but why stop there? What new challenges await you? Try a new adventure: *In the Jungle, Under the Sea, In the Wilderness, On the South Sea Islands, In the Himalayas, In the Desert,* and *At the North Pole.*

EXPLORERS WANTED!

ANSWERS from page 91

A. 4 B. 1 C. 2 D. 5 E. 3

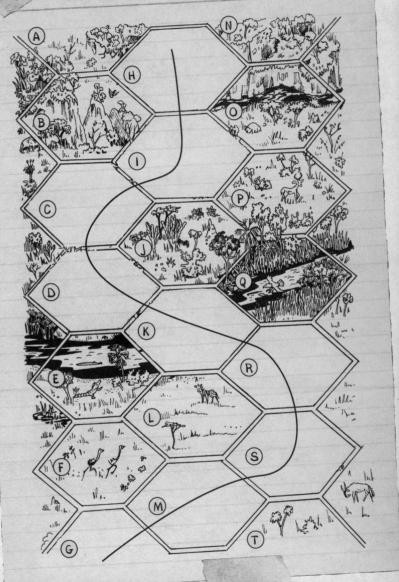

Your mission...

should you choose to accept it, is to find the legendary angel bird on Lunga Lunga Island.

Will you take up the challenge?

Explorers Wanted to:

- Explore the great Siberian wilderness
- Battle swarms of blood-sucking insects
- Brave the unpredictable weather conditions
- Canoe raging rivers and conquer fierce rapids
- Handle encounters with starving wolves and bears

Includes the author's own expedition notes and sketches!

EXPLORERS WANTED!

IN THE WILDERNESS

Simon Chapman

SO ... YOU WANT TO BE A WILDERNESS EXPLORER?

Do you want to ...
Brave the great **Siberian wilderness** ...?

Canoe **raging rapids** on wild white water ...?

Avoid being eaten by **bears, wolves, and wolverines** ...?
If the answer to any of these questions is **YES**,
then this is the book for you. Read on ...

103

THIS BOOK GIVES you the low down on exploring the Siberian Taiga forests, an environment that has extremes of climate and is stacked with potentially lethal wildlife. You'll learn what you need to take and how to deal with the hazards, and you'll find out about some of the people who tried to explore there before you.

YOUR MISSION ...

should you choose to accept it, is to head up an expedition into the heart of the Siberian wilderness — in search of a giant meteorite crater.

June 30, 1908, Tunguska, Eastern Siberia. A lump of rock from outer space the size of a tennis court zoomed into the Earth's atmosphere and exploded mid-air above the Siberian taiga, like an atom bomb going off. Trees were knocked flat for miles around and the noise of the explosion could be heard hundreds of kilometers away. But, what happened to the meteorite? Did it vaporize or did it smack into the ground, creating an enormous crater? Recently, a light plane ferrying a survey party to an oil-drilling station near the River Gorbushka reported strange things.

The pilot had become lost in a bank of low
cloud and when he dipped his plane to get
a better view, he realized he was lost.
What's more, his compass kept swinging
around. It would not point North. Circling
round he spotted a circular bowl-like
area amongst the forested hills.
A meteorite impact crater?

Now you've decided to go there, to locate the
impact site, and perhaps even find a piece
of the meteorite that you believe caused it.

Time to set the scene . . .

Let's find out some vital facts about Siberia and its environment before the mission gets under way.

The Taiga is a vast coniferous forest, stretching all the way from Finland across the Eurasian continent to the Pacific Ocean. The forest is bigger even than the Amazon rainforest in South America, and nearly all of it lies within just one country – Russia. This is the great Siberian wilderness.

THE GREAT SIBERIAN WILDERNESS.

TAIGA FOREST

Across the Pacific, the forest carries on across Alaska and Canada. Many of the creatures found there are the same, though they may have different names.

Siberian name		North American name
Wapiti	⟷	Elk
Elk	⟷	Moose
Wolf	⟷	Wolf
Brown Bear	⟶	Grizzly bear

So what is the Siberian Wilderness like? This depends on what time of year it is. The big thing to understand is that the climate here has two characters.

A short, hot, insect-ridden summer and a freezing, snowbound winter. Some parts of Eastern Siberia have the largest temperature range of anywhere in the world; up to a positively tropical 38°C in June and July and down to a chilly -68°C in the cold, dark winter.

WINTER

SUMMER

So close to the Artic, the hours of daylight are short by December. It's dark (dim even at midday), bitingly cold and, unless you know where to look or are prepared to dig through the snow, there is no food and hardly any animals. Many of them have either found a sheltered place to hibernate, or have moved away until the weather gets warmer.

So . . . summertime and the living is easy? No. It can snow even then. It can be fine all morning then there can be a blizzard by lunchtime. This will make it extra difficult to choose what gear to take with you.

You've decided to set off in the summer — the best time for an expedition. The rivers are high and fast-flowing with the snow that melted in the spring, and all the plants are growing full on in the few months before the cold weather returns. Bright-green new needle leaves have grown on the larches and birches, and the air is warm, humid, and buzzing with insects.

Away from the sunlit glades, the trees are tightly packed and it's gloomy and dim.

The forest floor is covered in moss, fuzzy lichens, and occasionally ferns among the fallen branches and pine needles. Pushing your way forward, you're up against more trunks, more moss, more of the same. It's clear you're going to need some sort of plan to navigate your way through this endless forest or else you're going to get yourself very lost.

Suddenly . . . a branch snaps behind you. You spin around. What could it be?

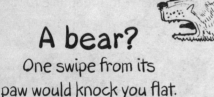

A bear?
One swipe from its paw would knock you flat. Then you're easy meat.

A ravenous wolf?
And where there's one, there's usually a whole pack.

An elk?
You won't want to tangle with antlers like those when the bulls blood is up in mating season.

Perhaps a wolverine?

It probably wouldn't attack you while you were upright and healthy, but what if you injured yourself?

Or is it just a dead branch dislodged by the wind in the treetops, tumbling down to Earth?

Looking up, you can see the treetops swaying. Clouds have blown across the sun and already you can feel the temperature drop. The mosquitoes and deer ticks are biting. The weather could be turning. Do you have enough food, cold-weather gear, or the equipment to improvise what you'll need with the resources you find around you?

Are you properly equipped?

About the author

Writer and broadcaster Simon Chapman is a self-confessed jungle addict, making expeditions whenever he can. His travels have taken him to tropical forests all over the world, from Borneo and Irian Jaya to the Amazon.

The story of his search for a mythical giant ape in the Bolivian rainforest, *The Monster of the Madidi*, was published in 2001. He has also had numerous articles and illustrations published in magazines in Britain and the United States, including *Wanderlust*, *BBC Wildlife*, and *South American Explorer*, and has written and recorded for BBC Radio 4, and lectured on the organization of jungle expeditions at the Royal Geographical Society, of which he is a fellow. When not exploring, Simon lives with his wife and his two young children in Lancaster, England, where he teaches high school physics.